Surprising
Things

We Do for
Beauty

Monika Davies

Consultants

Timothy Rasinski, Ph.D.
Kent State University

Lori Oczkus, M.A.
Literacy Consultant

Publishing Credits

Rachelle Cracchiolo, M.S.Ed., *Publisher*

Conni Medina, M.A.Ed., *Managing Editor*

Dona Herweck Rice, *Series Developer*

Emily R. Smith, M.A.Ed., *Content Director*

Stephanie Bernard/Noelle Cristea, M.A.Ed., *Editors*

Robin Erickson, *Senior Graphic Designer*

The TIME logo is a registered trademark of TIME Inc. Used under license.

Image Credits: p.11 Photo by Sue Hwang; p. 17 ullstein bild/ullstein bild via Getty Images; p. 21 ClassicStock/Alamy Stock Photo; p. 24 Zoonar GmbH/Alamy Stock Photo; p. 26 Koichi Kamoshida/Getty Images; pp. 34-35 China Photos/Getty Images; pp. 36-37 Eye Ubiquitous/UIG via Getty Images; pp. 38-39 NurPhoto/NurPhoto via Getty Images; p. 40 Public Domain image from Physiology for young people adapted to intermediate classes and common schools; p. 41 Hulton Archive/Getty Images; p. 42 Musée du Louvre, Dist. RMN-Grand Palais/Christian Decamps/Art Resource; p. 43 Thilo Parg/Wikimedia Commons License: CC BY-SA 3.0; p. 44 Maher Attar/Sygma via Getty Images; p. 45 The Getty Center, Object 144005, Digital image courtesy of the Getty's Open Content Program; p. 45 O'Reilly, Samuel F., inventor. United States Patent No. 464,801, dated December 8, 1891; p. 49 TOONMAN_blchin/Flickr License: Creative Commons BY-SA 3.0; p. 59 Photo by Kristen Lee; all other images from iStock and/or Shutterstock

Notes: The beauty techniques described throughout this book are for informational purposes only. Do not attempt to re-create these treatments or techniques. All companies and/or products mentioned in this book are registered trademarks of their respective owners or developers and are used in this book strictly for editorial purposes. No commercial claim to their use is made by the author or the publisher.

Teacher Created Materials

5301 Oceanus Drive
Huntington Beach, CA 92649-1030
http://www.tcmpub.com

ISBN 978-1-4938-3636-9

© 2017 Teacher Created Materials, Inc.

Table of Contents

Unconventional Approaches 4

Digging into Makeup Bags 6

Wild & Stylin' Hair through the Ages . . . 16

Reviewing Surprising Spas 24

Particular Profiles 32

A Timeline of Tattoos 42

Unique Facial Piercings 50

Complex Beauty 56

Glossary 58

Index 60

Check It Out! 62

Try It! 63

About the Author 64

Unconventional Approaches

People have done some pretty surprising things in the name of beauty. Glance through any style magazine and you'll find no lack of creative beauty routines to try. A quick Internet search will show eye-popping photos of the most bizarre ways people have enhanced their looks over the years.

Around the world, beauty fanatics have smeared their faces with **dehydrated** bird droppings and willingly stuck needles through their skin to wear jewelry. Rewind history, and you'll glimpse sky-high hair and eye shadow made of ground-up gemstones.

Beauty itself is a weird idea. The perception of beauty, of course, varies from person to person and culture to culture. Our idea of beauty reflects our lifestyle and values. Learning more about another culture's interpretation of what makes people beautiful gives meaningful insight into that culture's way of life.

Settle in, and investigate some of the most intriguing beauty practices—both ancient and current—around the world.

Is It Art?

Is a tattoo that winds and weaves a tale on a person's spine considered art? How about a face carefully painted with makeup? If we think of these beauty practices as art forms, does that change our opinions of their values?

Digging into Makeup Bags

Examining a makeup bag from another country—or another time—is a fascinating glimpse into a lifestyle different from one's own. Let's take a look to see what people have tucked into their cosmetic totes.

Korea

Two Cleansers

Many Koreans take pride in having flawless complexions, a direct result of a 10-step (yes, 10!) skin-care routine. The process begins with an oil-based cleanser, followed with a foaming cleanser. Koreans are gentle with their faces, using circular motions to cleanse a day's grime away.

Essence

Uniquely Korean, essence is a highly concentrated liquid. Full of beneficial properties, such as **glycerin**, essence hydrates your skin. A staple in the Asian beauty regime, essence is said to promote a wrinkle-free complexion.

Sheet Masks

While sheet masks can make you look like a mummy, Koreans swear by this unique skin-care solution. Sheet masks are treasure troves of skin-friendly vitamins. Letting the mask settle on your face allows the vitamins to absorb, ideally giving you the glow that's advertised!

Kimchi

The famous saying "you are what you eat" is also a part of Korean skin care. Kimchi is a beloved Korean superfood. This spicy fermented cabbage is loaded with **antioxidants**, which create a clear complexion.

A Lucrative Market

In 2014, the world's spending on cosmetics was a robust $460 billion, and that number continues to climb.

THINK LINK

In Asian countries, there is an emphasis on having pale skin, and many beauty products are created to brighten and lighten the complexion. However, Americans tend to idolize a tan complexion and spend their dollars on self-tanners.

- Why do you think the ideal complexions in American and Asian cultures are so different?
- What are some beauty ideals from around the world that directly contrast with your country's own?
- What kind of cultural influences affect these beauty ideals?

India

Coconut Oil

In India, as in many places, beauty secrets for both men and women are passed from one generation to the next, ensuring traditions live on through the family tree. This holds true for coconut oil, which is responsible for Indian women's proudest feature—lush hair. Grab a scoop of coconut oil in your hands and work it through your hair. Leave the oil on overnight, and shampoo the next day. This is guaranteed to leave you with a soft and smooth mane.

Rose Water

History's princesses reportedly used rose water for its special qualities. While rose water has a simple ingredient list, the liquid holds its own as a soothing, firming skin beautifier and a sweet mood-booster. Red, inflamed skin has met its ultimate enemy.

Turmeric

Yellow turmeric powder, native to India, can be found on both kitchen and bathroom shelves. Mostly used to spice up dishes, turmeric is also believed to help with common colds and indigestion. In the beauty world, turmeric is a job juggler. It is alternatively known as a skin healer, an anti-aging wizard, and a great foe of oily skin.

Gram Flour

Also known as *besan*, gram flour is the go-to **exfoliating** agent in India. Gram flour is made of chickpeas and can transform a dull complexion to one that glows.

Haldi Ceremony

Turmeric (*haldi*) is the superstar of a traditional bridal ceremony in India. On the morning of the wedding, both bridal partners are covered in turmeric paste to brighten their complexions for the ceremony, while also keeping evil spirits at bay.

Mexico

Avocado

At first glance, avocado might seem like an odd choice if you're used to seeing it used in guacamole. However, avocado is used in Mexico as a way to repair dry and damaged hair. Not only do avocados provide healthy fat when eaten, but the oil found in the them can also act as a deep conditioner to restore moisture and shine to your locks.

Tepezcohuite Tree

Dubbed Mexico's "skin tree," the tepezcohuite has all the signs of being a miracle worker. Renowned for its ability to **regenerate** skin, the tree's extract has quite an impressive résumé. It is said to have the ability to combat and treat wrinkles, acne, scars, burns, and other skin ailments.

Teaspoon

No need to look further than the kitchen drawer for a go-to eyelash curler! A teaspoon is a unique way to curl eyelashes. Here's how:

- Cup the teaspoon over the eyelid, with the bottom edge of the spoon resting horizontally at the root of the lashes.

- Hold the spoon in place and use your thumb or index finger to press the lashes against the back of the spoon.

- Holding the lashes, drag the teaspoon up and out to create an upward curl.

Great Grapes

Chile also uses its country's plants as **ingenious** cosmetic solutions. Chileans are fond of mashing up red grapes with flour and using this blend as a face mask to banish dead skin and leave their complexions smooth.

Ancient Egypt

Kohl

The ancient Egyptians' kohl-lined cat eyes are a look people replicate today. Aside from a glamorous look, there were some sensible reasons for keeping kohl in their bags. Research says the lead-based kohl would have mixed with moisture from the eyes, and the combination would have had anti-bacterial properties. A fantastic bonus for the perfect smoky eye!

Red Ochre

This finely ground powder was responsible for the ancient Egyptians' red puckers. Red **ochre** only needs some water to turn into a cosmetic paste. The red paste would then be carefully dabbed onto lips, creating a cherry-colored smile.

Malachite

Grind up shiny malachite, and you have a do-it-yourself, green eye shadow. This type of copper ore produces some vibrant greenery, a nice complement to kohl-lined eyes.

Henna

Are you in the market for naturally tinted yellow and orange fingernails? The ancient Egyptians would have passed you their heaps of henna to help your nails achieve that yellow-orange hue. Henna was also used as a natural way to dye hair.

Cleopatra's Bath Hour

The infamous ancient Egyptian queen regularly bathed in milk—donkey milk, to be specific. Rumor has it that over 700 donkeys were needed to produce enough milk to fill her tub.

illustration of Cleopatra

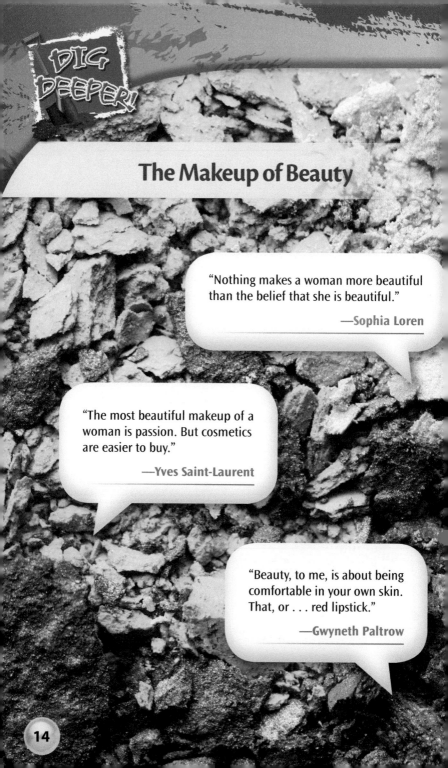

The Makeup of Beauty

"Nothing makes a woman more beautiful than the belief that she is beautiful."

—Sophia Loren

"The most beautiful makeup of a woman is passion. But cosmetics are easier to buy."

—Yves Saint-Laurent

"Beauty, to me, is about being comfortable in your own skin. That, or . . . red lipstick."

—Gwyneth Paltrow

"I love the confidence that makeup gives me."

—Tyra Banks

"Treat your makeup like jewelry for the face. Play with colors, shapes, structure—it can transform you."

—Francois Nars

Respond to the following questions:

- What do you think Sophia Loren means?
- How can a person be comfortable in his or her skin?
- In what ways can makeup can give someone confidence?
- How has Francois Nars used a simile?

Wild & Stylin' Hair through the Ages

People have spent decades fascinated with the colored strands that pop out from their heads. We put our hair through merry torture, forcing our manes to meet razors that shred, hot irons that scorch, and combs that are composed of sharp teeth. Hair strands are regularly dipped and dyed in a rainbow palette of shades, then braided, crimped, or curled to the exact measurement of the latest hair craze.

In other words, we have hardly given our hair a break—and that's the fun of it all! In honor of our hair devotion, here's a look at some of the wildest hairstyles over the last few centuries.

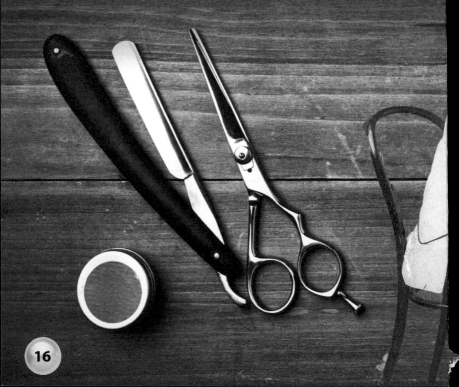

Queue

This hairstyle for men has historical significance that is anchored in the year 1644. This was the year when the Manchus, who were known for the hairstyle, overthrew the Han-ruled Ming dynasty. To exert their influence, the Manchus commanded that every man should also wear the queue hairstyle. The grim saying "lose your hair or lose your head" ensured Han men pulled out their razors and shaved their hair. The queue became a sign of submission and a sad reminder of how appearances can sometimes speak volumes.

Regular Upkeep

The queue required regular shaving to maintain its distinct shape. The front and sides were shaved, while the long strands at the back were braided.

Le Pouf

The sky-high pouf, seen on page 19, the go-to hairstyle for Marie Antoinette and her court in the eighteenth century, was a tricky style to maintain. A wire frame was used to expand the hair up, up, up. The pouf was then topped with the lady's choice of ornamentation.

Ladies might have made it their personal missions to outdo their friends, since the decorations started relatively tame—colorful feathers and jewels—and went to absolutely fantastical. It wasn't uncommon to see a lady sprouting vegetables, model ships, and even live birds from her head!

Powdered Hair

Open an average American wallet and there's a good chance George Washington—in full wig glory—is staring up at you from the dollar bill. Or *is* it a wig?

Patriots were not interested in keeping wigs in their hair closets, as it reminded them of the British. (There were definitely hard feelings between the two countries at the time.) So Washington achieved his commanding look using his own **bona fide** hair. The hairdo needed styling help from a **copious** amount of white hair powder. He would then cap off his mini ponytail with a little black bag wrapped around the base. This was the best strategy to keep a white powdery snowfall from coating his shoulders!

The Price of Extravagance

There's no denying *le pouf* was the height of sophistication in 1770s France; however, it came at a cost. The pouf required hours of prep work, so the style was hardly washed, causing **vermin** to hide and multiply in the hair. Casually napping on a bed was also out of the question, as women wearing the pouf had to sleep in a half-sitting position with their hair fully cushioned.

Marcel Wave

In 1872, Francois Marcel was responsible for the creation of a popular instrument of hair torture. The first curling iron on the market was rather high maintenance, requiring heating over a gas burner. To top it off, the iron was incredibly **temperamental**. Too hot, and the iron would burn the hair; too cool, and the wave wouldn't set. The Marcel wave (seen to the right) added an iconic flair to the 1920s hair movement, creating deep, even waves in the popular flapper bobs.

Victory Rolls

When the 1920s bob fell out of style, "victory rolls" began to rule hair trends. Loose curls formed the base of the hairstyle, while two large rolls of hair outlined the letter V at the top of the head.

Victory rolls were named after a World War II fighter-plane maneuver. The style quickly became a way to honor soldiers, as well as to celebrate the American victories in the war. The rolls also kept hair off the face—a perfect blend of patriotism and practicality!

Un*flap*pable

The flapper bob was exceptionally popular during the 1920s, a decade framed by roaring rebellion. Women wanted to chop off their long locks that hung with the weight of tradition. Many hairdressers refused to cut the new "bob" style, so **enterprising** ladies turned to barber shops for their new short dos.

Pipe Cleaner Clips

During World War II, all metal was needed for the war effort, and metal **barrettes** were suddenly out of commission. Women looked for creative solutions to keep their curls in place and turned to pipe cleaners as the new "hair clip" of choice.

The Five-Point Cut

The brainchild of Vidal Sassoon, the five-point cut first arrived in 1965. It was a sleek and cropped style, where the nape of the hair fell into a W shape. The final two **precise** points perfectly framed the face.

The swingy ease of the five-point cut—just a shake of the head to style—made the cut super popular. It was especially useful for women heading into the work force. During the feminist movement, the cut spelled authority and was a clear movement away from the curls of the past.

Dreadlocks

To see what some people consider the world's most incredible dreadlocks, hop over to Namibia and meet the women of the Himba tribe. Their eye-catching dreadlocks are an earthy red color, each with a fluffy tail of goat hair. These women maintain their dreadlocks' shape with an age-old recipe of butter and ground ochre called *otjize*.

Himba women spend time grooming their hair in the morning. At night, they sleep on wooden pillows to keep the dreadlocks undamaged. The dreadlocks also act as sun protection and insect repellent thanks to the application of the *otjize* mixture so **painstakingly** applied—a truly multitasking, beautiful custom.

Mane Symbols

Himba dreadlocks are styled in different ways to symbolize the different stages of a Himba woman's life. An animal skin headdress pinned to the top of the head tells that the wearer is already wed or has had her first child.

Namibian woman with dreadlocks

23

Reviewing Surprising Spas

Spas provide a menu of beauty remedies guaranteed to raise eyebrows. Let's look at a few of the world's most unique and outlandish spa treatments.

Social Time

The appeal of the banya is not only its health-boosting properties. The iconic Russian bathhouse is also a social atmosphere where friends can get together to chat.

Banya

Location
Russia

Description
The banya is a classic Russian tradition. The banya experience begins with entrance into the *parilka*, where guests are surrounded by hot, humid steam. This wooden room is heated with water that is poured on piping hot rocks that have been prepped in a furnace.

This steam room takes things to the next level with its collection of *venik* (birch branches). The bundles of branches aren't there for decoration, though—you can use them to beat toxins from your body!

After this therapeutic branch beating, guests make their way to the nearby basseyn (ice-cold bath) for a shocking wake-up from the heat. To fully appreciate the health benefits of a Russian banya, guests should repeat this hot and cold pattern a few times.

Benefits
- sweat stress and toxins away
- fluctuation between hot and cold boosts the immune system

Review
The Russians say, "Бáня - мать вторáя," which essentially means "the banya is my second mother." That pretty much sums up my experience.

—*Spa-Sational89 reviewer*

Chocolate Escape Package

Location
Hershey, Pennsylvania

Description
The town of Hershey is home to the first modern chocolate factory. "The sweetest place on Earth" may be the best place for chocoholics to indulge in a spa.

This spa package may be calorie-free **decadence** at its finest. The signature package's focal points are a whipped cocoa bath and chocolate fondue wrap. But beware—your taste buds might water during the entire 3.5-hour process!

While covering yourself in chocolate sounds like an idea straight from Willy Wonka, this spa treatment has surprising benefits. The oil in cocoa butter makes for a moisturizing superstar. Dark chocolate's antioxidants may also slow down signs of aging.

Benefits
- increases happiness levels by smelling chocolate

- moisturizes and turns back the clock on aging

Review
I consider it an accomplishment that I didn't grab every bowl of chocolate treatment and run.

—*Sweet_Sweetie reviewer*

THINK LINK

- Why do you think people go to spas, aside from seeking beauty treatments?
- Which age group (if any) would be most likely to go to a spa, and why?
- How popular do you think spas are around the world? Would their clients likely be locals or tourists?

Fish Pedicures

Location

Southeast Asia

Description

Plunge your feet into an aquarium bursting with *Garra rufa*, tiny fish that have an appetite for dead skin. These fish, nicknamed "doctor fish," make sure your feet emerge flake-free. Don't worry—these toothless fish won't eat your toes for dinner; but, this treatment could be agony for anyone who's ticklish!

Fish pedicures are available in a variety of locations in Southeast Asia. Often, you will find them in night market pop-up spas with rock-bottom prices. However, fish pedicures do draw a fair deal of controversy. The potential risk of infection is something to take into account before dipping your toes in.

Benefits

- smooth feet achieved without a pumice stone
- temporary relief of the dead skin buildup caused by serious skin conditions

Review

Yes, the whole *my-feet-are-being-consumed-by-fish* thing did freak me out at first. But the whole time all I could think of was how much it tickled.

—*Feet_Feats reviewer*

Risky Business?

While the fish pedicure may have made its way over to the United States, it is banned in several states. The main concern is that there is no way to sanitize the fish between patients, which leads to health concerns.

Bird Poop Facials

Location

Japan

Description

No joke—this exclusive and sought-after beauty treatment is made out of nightingale droppings. Before the *ew!* factor hits too hard, it's good to know that the droppings are subjected to a pretty intense UV light exam. This dehydrates the droppings, thereby removing all bacteria. The end result is a fine powder worth mega money. The powder is then shipped worldwide, and various spas are happy to **pony up** cash to meet the powder's hefty price tag.

You're more likely to find this facial listed as the **Geisha** Facial®, an allusion to its Japanese origin story. Surfacing in the seventeenth century in Japan, this facial was used by geishas to battle skin damage from their thick, heavy makeup. Now, the facial is on its second life as a deluxe treat for adventurous spa-goers.

Benefits

- exfoliates and transforms dull skin, giving it a bright complexion
- is comparable to Botox® for its anti-aging properties

Review

It smells a little musty, but if you refuse to really contemplate what is being slathered on your face, you'll be fine.

—*Price_Is_No_Object reviewer*

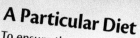

A Particular Diet

To ensure the nightingale droppings are 100 percent natural, the birds are fed only seeds and berries. Your facial is certified as vegan friendly.

Particular Profiles

Cultures constantly reshape their ideas of beauty. This sometimes translates into a literal reshaping of one's features. Body modification, permanently changing one's appearance, is one of the more extreme ways we approach beauty.

Often, the reason behind a traditional body-altering practice is rooted in cultural meaning. There can be fierce pressure to alter one's appearance simply for tradition's sake and often for family honor.

The Extension of a Neck

The Kayan people of Myanmar hold their heads high with what appear to be elongated necks, courtesy of brass rings. In Kayan culture, a long neck is a traditional symbol of beauty. The brass neck rings can be worn by a girl once she reaches the age of five. More rings are added as the girl matures.

In a way, the length of a Kayan woman's neck is based in illusion. Instead of stretching the neck, the weight of the rings pushes down on the collarbone muscles. This eventually compresses the rib cage, making it appear as if the Kayan women have longer necks.

A Weight on Their Shoulders

A full set of neck rings can weigh anywhere from 20–25 pounds (9–11 kilograms), though a full set is not common anymore. Despite the weight, the Kayan people truly believe the neck rings do not severely restrict movement throughout the day.

Foot Binding

For a **millennium**, the Chinese practiced foot binding, a painful custom that stunted the growth of a girl's feet while expanding her status. Hold one of the tiny shoes from the era of foot binding, and you may feel your toes curl in agony. It seems unimaginable that a human foot could fit into this **minuscule**, cramped space.

The binding process usually began when the girl was between four and six years old. All toes except the largest were broken and bound to the sole of the foot. The foot was then doubled in half and held together with a silk strip. As time went on, the bindings would grow tighter and tighter until the foot was no more than 3 to 4 inches (7.5 to 10 cm) long. In total, the grueling process took two years to complete.

Foot binding not only changed the shape of a foot, but it also altered a woman's **gait**. The way she walked became more **stilted**, confining her to a much smaller world. The practice continued, though, as tiny feet were a symbol of attractiveness and were the key to a woman successfully finding a husband. In the twentieth century, it fell out of favor.

STOP! THINK...

Cosmetic procedures are common types of body modification. Surgical procedures require medical operations, while nonsurgical procedures are those that do not require surgery. Have a look at the number of procedures completed in the United States over the last two decades:

- How does the number of procedures completed today compare to 1997?

- Why do you think there has been a change in the numbers?

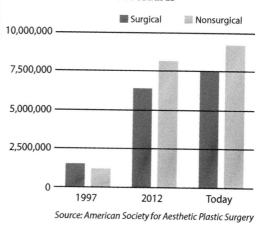

Cosmetic Procedures

■ Surgical ■ Nonsurgical

Source: American Society for Aesthetic Plastic Surgery

Permanent Marks of Status

You may have never seen tattoos quite like the ones proudly worn by the Māori of New Zealand. Uniquely designed by artists of the trade, the curved shapes and spirals wind around on faces. Every tattoo is unique. Its purpose is to communicate history and stature without a word spoken.

Traditionally, *tā moko* was etched onto the face with a chisel made of **albatross** bone and **pigment** from a tree. It is no surprise that the process was incredibly painful. However, at the turn of the twentieth century, tattoo needles became more commonly used in the procedure.

Since there is no dedicated road map for a Māori facial tattoo, the tattoo takes on a life of its own. The wearer's history from the father's side is imprinted on the left side of his or her face, while the mother's history is on the right. Typically, Māori men have full facial tattoos, while Māori women generally only ink their chins, lips, and nostrils.

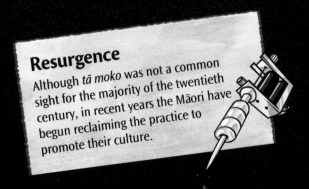

Resurgence

Although *tā moko* was not a common sight for the majority of the twentieth century, in recent years the Māori have begun reclaiming the practice to promote their culture.

A Smile with Bite

The Mentawai tribe in Indonesia sharpens a woman's smile using a file . . . without anything to dull the pain. It's a little startling to glimpse the pointed ridges of a Mentawai woman's sharpened smile. The tribe believes that the sharpening of teeth is a key component of female beauty. In this culture, it is also believed that the painful sharpening balances the body and soul.

The instruments for the procedure are **crude**, and no **anesthetic** is used during the sharpening process. The **shaman** of the village uses a sharp chisel to create the new shapes, filing the edges to a sharp point. Afterwards, women are usually given green bananas to bite upon to help numb the pain.

As the modern world has crept in, the practice is now optional and voluntary. However, a woman's motivation to sharpen her teeth can be complicated and subject to outside influences. For example, a National Geographic documentary showed that the soon-to-be chief of a tribe had asked his wife to have her teeth sharpened to increase her beauty. She did as she was asked.

Teeth & Tattoos

The Mentawai tribe is also known for its distinctive tattoos. Much like in the tooth-sharpening tradition, people are inked using more traditional tools. A needle laced with ink is pounded into the skin.

The Dangers of Corsets: Myth or Fact?

There is debate over whether tight-lacing a **corset** actually changes the anatomy of the body over time. In recent years, the "waist training" corset, which supposedly trains your waist to a slimmer version of itself, gained popularity. Most physicians do not recommend these corsets, stating that these support garments may make breathing more difficult, but more notably, they simply don't work.

So, myth or fact—will corsets dangerously alter one's body? Consider the following:

- ◎ Looking at the comparison picture below, do you think the image is telling the truth? Could a corset actually change the internal organs and produce that slender of a waist?

- ◎ Many advertisements for cosmetics or beauty procedures like the one to the right make claims they can't support. How do we recognize false claims?

- ◎ Why do you think people fall prey to advertisements that promise the impossible?

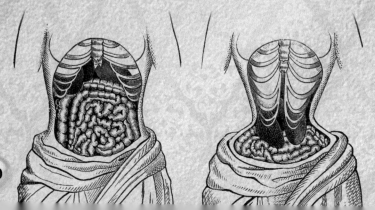

THE RIBS AND TIGHT-LAC

IN WELL-SHAPED CORSETS.

HE difference both in comfort and health that there is between a badly-shaped and a well-shaped corset is very great. The former the bottom of nearly all the ills that are generally considered as ially belonging to corset wearing, and reformers generally condemn quite rightly) the wearing of corsets on account of their knowledge g been gleaned from the results of wearing badly-shaped corsets. corset that varies little in size all the way down will, if tightly- compress the thorax and reduce the breathing capacity very much ut producing a small waist, or even a fashionable-looking figure.

of room in essential places with the greatest appea The corsets should be fashioned on the double cur beauty) principle. They should curve outwards ab room to the thorax, and inwards at the waist to gi following illustrations are designed to show the effe corsets on the ribs.

Fig. 1 shows the natural form of a young lady wi The thorax is shown inside the outline of the body, a through the smallest part of the waist, with the spinal

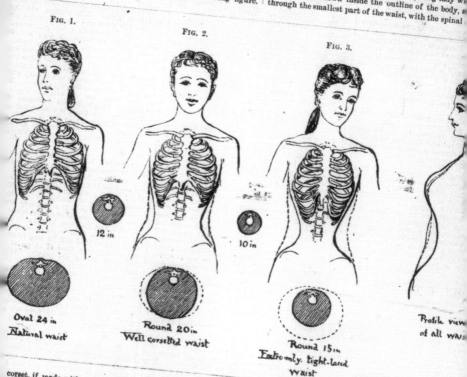

FIG. 1.

FIG. 2.

FIG. 3.

Oval 24 in
Natural waist

12 in

Round 20 in
Well corsetted waist

10 in

Round 15 in
Extremely tight-laced
waist

Profile view
of all wai

corset, if made with straight sides, will compress the ribs oportion to the effect of slenderness produced.
er hand, a well-shaped corset will give a great appearance e slenderness to the figure without being uncomfortable, or g to be really tightly laced, and it will not produce the ills that a badly-shaped one will assuredly do.
been any number of illustrations published of the effects g on the ribs by badly-shaped corsets, but not the effect ell-shaped corsets—namely, those that give the maximum

XVII.

The waist is oval in shape, with its greatest width from side about 8¾ in., and front to back of under 6¾ in.
Fig. 2 shows a similarly formed young lady, but with her wa to 20 in. If the reduction is done gradually, lasting over a y inconvenience or unpleasant tightness will be felt, and 20 in. i presentable little waist, and looks fashionable small, particularly round, as shown in the section below. The width h vs of waist would be about 6¾ in., or nearly the same epth natural 24 in. waist. The dotted lines both in the f y and

A Timeline of Tattoos

History is rich in evidence that tattooing has existed since early man roamed the earth. Take a trip with us through the years as we explore the history of tattoos from around the world and across the ages.

Approximately 3200 BC

Ötzi the Iceman was uncovered in 1991, the oldest tattooed archaeological find. His body was found with 61 tattoos, all of which were lines in his skin, colored with charcoal. Researchers have guessed they marked acupuncture spots. Acupuncture involves placing needles into a person's skin to relieve pain or cure illness. This may mean old Ötzi was not in the greatest of health.

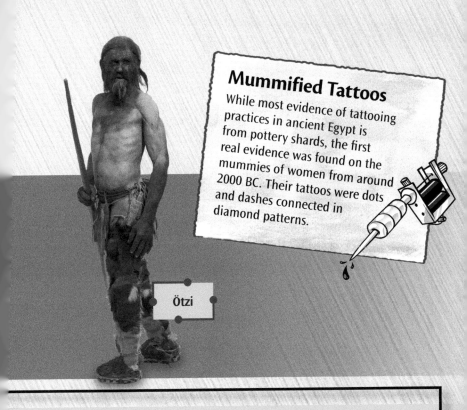

Mummified Tattoos

While most evidence of tattooing practices in ancient Egypt is from pottery shards, the first real evidence was found on the mummies of women from around 2000 BC. Their tattoos were dots and dashes connected in diamond patterns.

Ötzi

4000–1450 BC

There is definite evidence that the ancient Egyptians were fond of tattooing. The earliest signs are tattooed individuals found on pottery from that age, while tattooing tools from 1450 BC were also found in northern Egypt.

Tattoos from this era were typically found on women, and it is unclear why this was the case. One possible theory is that women were tattooed to protect themselves from difficult pregnancies and births. A common tattoo was a series of dots spread in a net-like fashion on the abdomen. When a woman was pregnant, the dots would expand.

Greek and Roman Times (500 BC–AD 400)

The art of tattooing took a distressing, negative turn in Greek and Roman times. Tattoos were used as a form of punishment and a marker for both slaves and criminals. This ensured that if a slave or criminal attempted to escape, he or she could be quickly reclaimed. Authorities would often tattoo criminals' foreheads with their crimes—a cruel way to make sure their pasts would haunt them for the rest of their lives.

Edo Period (1603–1867)

Tattoos have a long and uneasy history in Japan. During the Edo period, people got full bodysuits of tattoos, called *wabori*. It was also around this time that tattoos and criminal activity became linked. Japanese convicts were marked with **penal** tattoos to (negatively) stand out in a crowd.

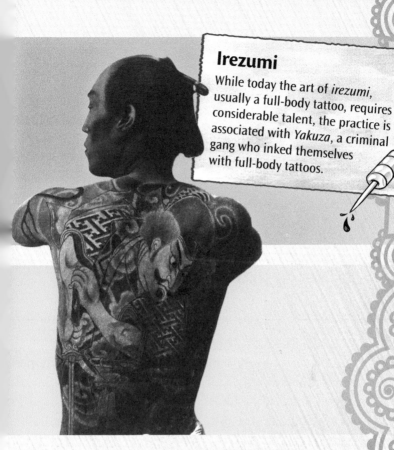

Irezumi

While today the art of *irezumi*, usually a full-body tattoo, requires considerable talent, the practice is associated with *Yakuza*, a criminal gang who inked themselves with full-body tattoos.

1769

When English Captain James Cook arrived in Tahiti, he found that the Polynesian culture encouraged bold tattooing. They named the beautiful coloring on their skin *tatau*. The word *tatau* eventually morphed into the word we use today, *tattoo*.

1800 and Onward

Sailors began to opt for tattoos to document their travels. An anchor meant they had crossed the Atlantic, a turtle indicated their ships had crossed the equator, and a dragon told of a voyage into Asia.

1846

Martin Hildebrandt, a German immigrant, set up shop in lower Manhattan. His tattoo parlor was the first of its kind in the United States.

1891

Samuel O'Reilly, a New Yorker, nabbed the **patent** for the first electric tattoo machine. O'Reilly built upon one of Thomas Edison's designs—the autographic printer. It was originally a handheld device. The needle moved rapidly and punctured tiny holes into a piece of paper. It was one of Edison's designs that fell flat. O'Reilly brilliantly **tweaked** the concept by adding ink. His idea revolutionized the tattooing world.

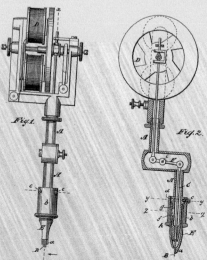

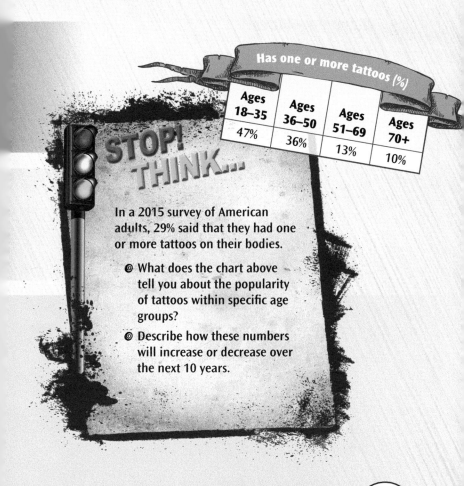

STOP! THINK...

In a 2015 survey of American adults, 29% said that they had one or more tattoos on their bodies.

- What does the chart above tell you about the popularity of tattoos within specific age groups?
- Describe how these numbers will increase or decrease over the next 10 years.

1940s

During World War II, the tattoo industry experienced a boom. As the sizes of the American army and navy doubled and tripled, more soldiers and sailors acquired tattoos.

1950s

Tattoos were still viewed as the domain of sailors and soldiers. The buttoned-up, conservative 1950s society frowned upon the inking practice. The art of tattooing went underground and became less commonplace.

1961

New York City banned tattooing, announcing it was "unlawful for any person to tattoo a human being." The city pointed to a recent, minor outbreak of **hepatitis B** as the reason behind the ban. However, whether tattoo salons were the true culprits behind the outbreak is debatable even today.

1970s

Janis Joplin, an iconic rock 'n' roll star, had a bracelet design inked on her wrist. Joplin was one of the first celebrities to show off a tattoo. The design was seen as a symbol of female strength. Slowly, more feminine tattoos began emerging in popular culture.

1997

New York legalized tattooing in February, and the city then hosted its first tattoo convention in May.

Present

Tattoos have gained mainstream acceptance. There are now many reasons that adults permanently ink their skin, but in this day and age, one of the strongest reasons to get a tattoo is as an artful form of self-expression.

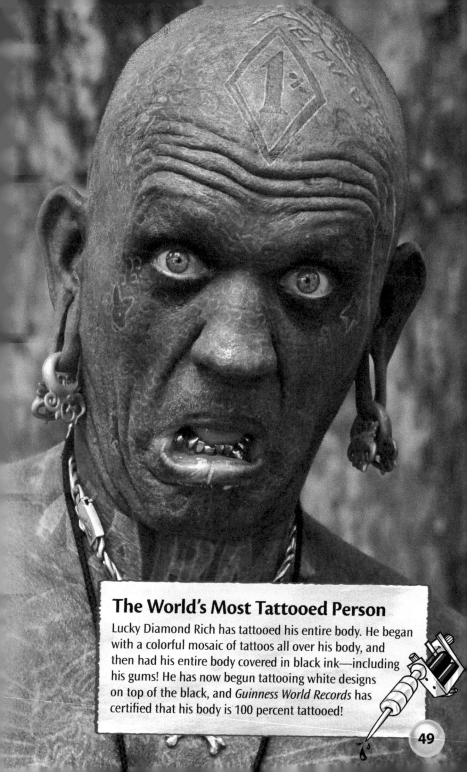

The World's Most Tattooed Person

Lucky Diamond Rich has tattooed his entire body. He began
with a colorful mosaic of tattoos all over his body, and
then had his entire body covered in black ink—including
his gums! He has now begun tattooing white designs
on top of the black, and *Guinness World Records* has
certified that his body is 100 percent tattooed!

49

Unique Facial Piercings

Some of the most surprising piercings are not appealing to everyone. That being said, it is mind-boggling to consider the number of options that exist. Just like tattooing, piercing comes with cultural, religious, and status implications.

Eyeball Jewelry

Requiring surgery and steady nerves, eyeball jewelry adds a literal twinkle to your eye. During the 10-minute process, a small **incision** is made in the outer membrane of the eye, using scissors. This tiny slit is where the jewelry is then delicately inserted. The conversation-starting piercing is removable but only with professional help. While the procedure has made waves in New York and Europe, you'll have to save a lot of money to get it done. This daring piercing comes with a $3,000 price tag.

Nath

Many women in India have their noses pierced when they turn 16, the traditional age of marriage. This is to honor the Hindu goddess of marriage, Parvati. On her wedding day, the bride wears an **ornate** *nath*, a sizable nose ring of gold or silver attached to the ear or hair. These stunning nose rings are a symbol of marriage. Depending on the location in India, a woman continues to wear her nose ring until her husband dies.

A Love of Piercings

Americans really love earlobe studs. It is estimated that around 83 percent of all Americans have had their ears pierced.

Which Nostril?

In India, either nostril may be pierced.
However, it is believed that piercing the left
nostril will help ease the stress of childbirth.

Lip Plates (dhebi a tugoin)

At first blush, you might mistake lip plates for a form of suffering. However, this distinctive piercing holds a wealth of meaning for Ethiopia's Mursi tribe.

When a girl turns 15 or 16, her mother cuts the girl's lower lip, inserting a wooden plug to hold the cut open as it heals. As the months go by, progressively larger plugs are inserted. This continues until the lip is stretched wide enough to hold a pottery plate, one the girl has colored and designed herself.

The lip plate is a symbol of female maturity in the Mursi tribe, and the piercing indicates the woman can now have children. Often, the lip is pierced a year before the girl reaches marrying age. The decision to pierce her lip is left entirely up to the girl, and many women marry without piercing their lips.

While the piercing is likely painful for the first several months, the pain eventually disappears. Although the lip plate does not greatly affect the woman's quality of life, it can slow her walking pace, as it sways with her steps.

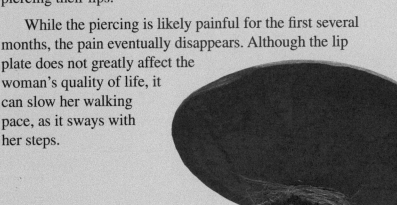

Plate Removal

Lip plates are removed to make talking, eating, and sleeping easier and more comfortable.

14 Different Ear Piercings

The earlobe stud is just the tip of the iceberg when it comes to ear piercings. Here are at least 14 different ways to pierce ears.

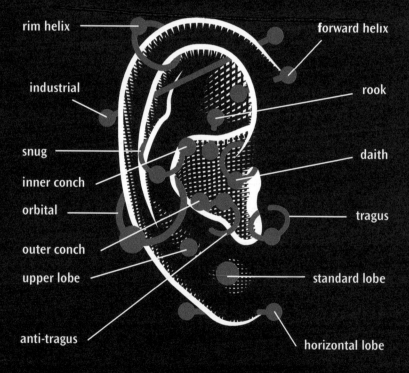

rim helix
forward helix
industrial
rook
snug
daith
inner conch
orbital
tragus
outer conch
upper lobe
standard lobe
anti-tragus
horizontal lobe

- Why do adults pierce their ears multiple times?
- How do ear piercings relate to ideas of beauty?

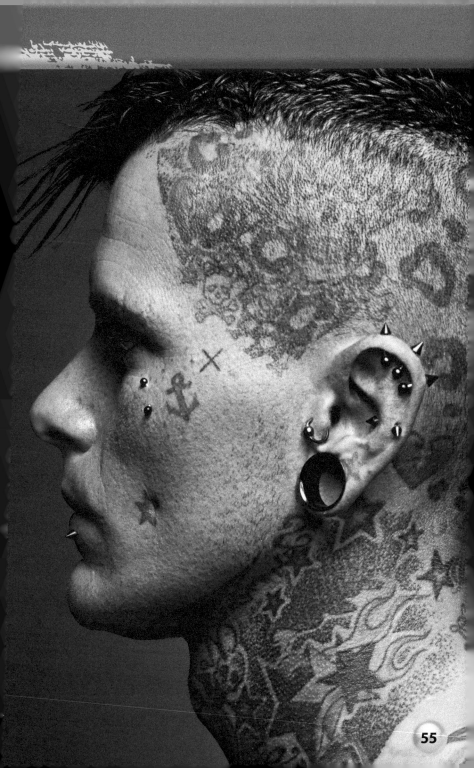

Complex Beauty

Defining beauty is complex and will always be subject to scrutiny. Things that seem surprising to others aren't strange to people or out of place within a given culture. Each culture derives their own meaning for the word *beautiful*.

Every culture, country, and person has different approaches to demonstrating beauty. Undoubtedly, beauty is a concept with many definitions. Those definitions change over the years, with new trends setting in. In a world of selfies and social media, it's even more important to focus on what can't be seen. Make sure your concept of beauty encompasses your character, your passion, and your values. And keep in mind that every person's definition of what makes someone beautiful grows and evolves with time. In the end, the most meaningful perspective will always be the one we determine for ourselves.

Mirror, Mirror on the Wall

We look into mirrors every day. But consider how our lives would change if we had no mirrors at all. Would it change how we see ourselves? Would it change how we see others?

Be your own kind of beautiful.

Glossary

albatross—large ocean bird with long wings

anesthetic—a substance that lessens pain

antioxidants—substances in foods that stop harmful chemical reactions

barrettes—decorative clips or bars used to hold hair in place

bona fide—genuine; real

concoction—something made by mixing different things together

copious—plentiful

corset—clothing worn by women to make their waists appear smaller

crude—very simple

decadence—unrestrained indulgence

dehydrated—something that has had its moisture removed

enterprising—resourceful

exfoliating—rubbing off dead skin cells

fluctuation—movement back and forth

gait—way of walking

geisha—a Japanese woman trained to entertain with song, dance, or conversation

glycerin—a liquid used in making medicine, food, soap, etc., that helps to moisturize

hepatitis B—a serious virus

incision—a cut

ingenious—clever

millennium—1,000 years

minuscule—extremely small

ochre—a mineral taken from the earth; yellow, red, or orange in color

ornate—decorative with plenty of detail and complexity

painstakingly—carefully done

patent—license for the rights of your invention so no one else can sell your idea

penal—relating to the prison system

pigment—natural coloring substance

pony up—to pay

precise—exact and accurate

regenerate—to regrow

shaman—a person who, in some cultures, is believed to use magic to cure disease

stilted—stiff and awkward

temperamental—unpredictable

tweaked—modified for improvement

vermin—small insects or animals

Index

Africa, 22

Antoinette, Marie, 18

banya, 24–25

Chile, 11

China 17, 34

Cleopatra, 12–13

corset, 40–41

cosmetic procedure, 35

dreadlocks, 22–23

Egypt, 12, 43

Ethiopia, 53

eyeball jewelry, 50

five-point cut, 22

flapper bob, 20

foot binding, 34

France, 18, 20

Geisha Facial, 30

Greece, 44

Guinness World Records, 49

Hershey, Pennsylvania, 26

Himba, 22

India, 8–9, 50–51

Indonesia, 39

irezumi, 45

Japan, 30, 44–45

Kayan, 32

Korea, 6–7

le pouf, 18–19

lip plate, 52–53

Lucky Diamond Rich, 49

Māori, 36–37

Marcel, Francois, 20

Mentawai, 39

Mexico, 10

Ming dynasty, 17

Mursi, 53

Myanmar, 32

Namibia, 22–23

nath, 50–51

neck stretching, 32–33

New York City, 46, 48, 50

New Zealand, 36

piercing, 50–51, 53–55

queue, 17

Rome, 44

Russia, 24–25

Sassoon, Vidal, 22

spas, 24, 26–28, 30

tā moko, 36–37

Tahiti, 45

tattoo, 4, 36, 39, 42–49

teeth sharpening, 38–39

United States, 29, 35, 46

victory rolls, 20

Yakuza, 45

Check It Out!

Books

Graydon, Shari. 2004. *In Your Face: The Culture of Beauty and You.* Annick Press.

Krull, Kathleen. 2011. *Big Wig: A Little History of Hair.* Arthur A. Levine Books.

Namioka, Lensey. 2000. *Ties that Bind, Ties that Break.* Laurel Leaf.

Westerfeld, Scott. 2011. *Uglies.* Simon Pulse.

Websites

Noroc, Mihaela. *The Atlas of Beauty.* http://www.theatlasofbeauty.com.

Southern Poverty Law Center. *Teaching Tolerance.* http://www.tolerance.org.

Try It!

Imagine you are designing a unique cultural tattoo like those of the Māori people. You will need to decide what traditions, celebrations, and/or beliefs you want to highlight in the tattoo.

- First, make a list of the cultural traditions in your family. What holidays or occasions do you celebrate? What traditional foods do you eat? What beliefs do you hold?
- Think about any artifacts your family holds dear. Do you have mementos or artifacts that have been passed down from one generation to the next? Are there traditional stories that you tell? Add these things to the list.
- Look at your list and highlight a few things that you can symbolize with a sketch. Perhaps there is a date that is important to your family/culture or an important word or phrase you would like to include in the tattoo. Consider any traditional colors that are used in your culture as well.
- Sketch and color your tattoo. Make sure to think about how large it will be and if it will be a single tattoo or several small ones combined.
- Once you've sketched the tattoo, write a detailed explanation of each element so that people of other cultures will understand the significance of the design.

About the Author

Monika Davies is a Canadian writer and traveler. She is a firm believer that red lipstick can solve most problems, and she thinks the most beautiful things in the world are pepperoni pizzas, a passport loaded with stamps, and her dog's smile. She has traveled to 34 countries and still finds the most beautiful part of any country to be its people. Davies graduated from the University of British Columbia with a bachelor of fine arts in creative writing.